THIS ADDRESS BOOK BELONG TO..

NAME

____

E-MAIL

____

ADDRESS

____

PHONE / MOBILE

____

SOCIAL MEDIA

____

Name

Address

Phone   Mobile
E-mail
Social Media
Birthday

~~~~~

Name

Address

Phone   Mobile
E-mail
Social Media
Birthday

~~~~~

Name

Address

Phone   Mobile
E-mail
Social Media
Birthday

Name

Address

Phone   Mobile

E-mail

Social Media

Birthday

Name

Address

Phone   Mobile

E-mail

Social Media

Birthday

Name

Address

Phone   Mobile

E-mail

Social Media

Birthday

Name

Address

Phone   Mobile

E-mail

Social Media

Birthday

Name

Address

Phone   Mobile

E-mail

Social Media

Birthday

Name

Address

Phone   Mobile

E-mail

Social Media

Birthday

A

Name

Address

Phone   Mobile

E-mail

Social Media

Birthday

Name

Address

Phone   Mobile

E-mail

Social Media

Birthday

Name

Address

Phone   Mobile

E-mail

Social Media

Birthday

Name

Address

Phone   Mobile

E-mail

Social Media

Birthday

Name

Address

Phone   Mobile

E-mail

Social Media

Birthday

Name

Address

Phone   Mobile

E-mail

Social Media

Birthday

Name
Address

Phone   Mobile
E-mail
Social Media
Birthday

~~~~~~~~

Name
Address

Phone   Mobile
E-mail
Social Media
Birthday

~~~~~~~~

Name
Address

Phone   Mobile
E-mail
Social Media
Birthday

Name

Address

Phone   Mobile

E-mail

Social Media

Birthday

~~~~~~~~~

Name

Address

Phone   Mobile

E-mail

Social Media

Birthday

~~~~~~~~~

Name

Address

Phone   Mobile

E-mail

Social Media

Birthday

B

Name

Address

Phone   Mobile
E-mail
Social Media
Birthday

Name

Address

Phone   Mobile
E-mail
Social Media
Birthday

Name

Address

Phone   Mobile
E-mail
Social Media
Birthday

Name

Address

Phone   Mobile

E-mail

Social Media

Birthday

Name

Address

Phone   Mobile

E-mail

Social Media

Birthday

Name

Address

Phone   Mobile

E-mail

Social Media

Birthday

C

Name

Address

Phone   Mobile
E-mail
Social Media
Birthday

Name

Address

Phone   Mobile
E-mail
Social Media
Birthday

Name

Address

Phone   Mobile
E-mail
Social Media
Birthday

Name

Address

C

Phone   Mobile

E-mail

Social Media

Birthday

~

Name

Address

Phone   Mobile

E-mail

Social Media

Birthday

~

Name

Address

Phone   Mobile

E-mail

Social Media

Birthday

Name

Address

Phone   Mobile

E-mail

Social Media

Birthday

Name

Address

Phone   Mobile

E-mail

Social Media

Birthday

Name

Address

Phone   Mobile

E-mail

Social Media

Birthday

Name

Address

Phone   Mobile

E-mail

Social Media

Birthday

~~~~~~~~~

Name

Address

Phone   Mobile

E-mail

Social Media

Birthday

~~~~~~~~~

Name

Address

Phone   Mobile

E-mail

Social Media

Birthday

D

Name

Address

Phone   Mobile

E-mail

Social Media

Birthday

Name

Address

Phone   Mobile

E-mail

Social Media

Birthday

Name

Address

Phone   Mobile

E-mail

Social Media

Birthday

Name

Address

Phone   Mobile

E-mail

Social Media

Birthday

~~~~~~~~~

Name

Address

Phone   Mobile

E-mail

Social Media

Birthday

~~~~~~~~~

Name

Address

Phone   Mobile

E-mail

Social Media

Birthday

D

Name

Address

Phone   Mobile

E-mail

Social Media

Birthday

~~~~~~~~

Name

Address

Phone   Mobile

E-mail

Social Media

Birthday

~~~~~~~~

Name

Address

Phone   Mobile

E-mail

Social Media

Birthday

Name

Address

Phone   Mobile

E-mail

Social Media

Birthday

~~~~~~~~~~

Name

Address

Phone   Mobile

E-mail

Social Media

Birthday

~~~~~~~~~~

Name

Address

Phone   Mobile

E-mail

Social Media

Birthday

Name

Address

Phone   Mobile

E-mail

Social Media

Birthday

Name

Address

Phone   Mobile

E-mail

Social Media

Birthday

Name

Address

Phone   Mobile

E-mail

Social Media

Birthday

Name

Address

Phone   Mobile

E-mail

Social Media

Birthday

~~~~~~~~

Name

Address

Phone   Mobile

E-mail

Social Media

Birthday

~~~~~~~~

Name

Address

Phone   Mobile

E-mail

Social Media

Birthday

E

Name

Address

Phone   Mobile

E-mail

Social Media

Birthday

~~~~~~~

Name

Address

Phone   Mobile

E-mail

Social Media

Birthday

~~~~~~~

Name

Address

Phone   Mobile

E-mail

Social Media

Birthday

Name

Address

Phone   Mobile

E-mail

Social Media

Birthday

~~~~~~~~

Name

Address

Phone   Mobile

E-mail

Social Media

Birthday

~~~~~~~~

Name

Address

Phone   Mobile

E-mail

Social Media

Birthday

Name

Address

Phone   Mobile

E-mail

Social Media

Birthday

~~~~~~~~~

Name

Address

Phone   Mobile

E-mail

Social Media

Birthday

~~~~~~~~~

Name

Address

Phone   Mobile

E-mail

Social Media

Birthday

Name

Address

Phone   Mobile

E-mail

Social Media

Birthday

~~~~~~~

Name

Address

Phone   Mobile

E-mail

Social Media

Birthday

~~~~~~~

Name

Address

Phone   Mobile

E-mail

Social Media

Birthday

Name

Address

Phone   Mobile

E-mail

Social Media

Birthday

Name

Address

Phone   Mobile

E-mail

Social Media

Birthday

Name

Address

Phone   Mobile

E-mail

Social Media

Birthday

Name

Address

Phone   Mobile

E-mail

Social Media

Birthday

G

~~~~~~~~~~

Name

Address

Phone   Mobile

E-mail

Social Media

Birthday

~~~~~~~~~~

Name

Address

Phone   Mobile

E-mail

Social Media

Birthday

G

Name

Address

Phone   Mobile

E-mail

Social Media

Birthday

~~~~~~~~

Name

Address

Phone   Mobile

E-mail

Social Media

Birthday

~~~~~~~~

Name

Address

Phone   Mobile

E-mail

Social Media

Birthday

Name

Address

Phone   Mobile

E-mail

Social Media

Birthday

~~~~~~~

Name

Address

Phone   Mobile

E-mail

Social Media

Birthday

~~~~~~~

Name

Address

Phone   Mobile

E-mail

Social Media

Birthday

Name

Address

Phone   Mobile

E-mail

G Social Media

Birthday

~~~~~~

Name

Address

Phone   Mobile

E-mail

Social Media

Birthday

~~~~~~

Name

Address

Phone   Mobile

E-mail

Social Media

Birthday

Name

Address

Phone   Mobile

E-mail

Social Media

Birthday   H

~~~~~~~

Name

Address

Phone   Mobile

E-mail

Social Media

Birthday

~~~~~~~

Name

Address

Phone   Mobile

E-mail

Social Media

Birthday

H

Name

Address

Phone   Mobile

E-mail

Social Media

Birthday

~~~~~~~~

Name

Address

Phone   Mobile

E-mail

Social Media

Birthday

~~~~~~~~

Name

Address

Phone   Mobile

E-mail

Social Media

Birthday

Name ____

Address ____

____

____

Phone _______________________ Mobile __________________

E-mail ____

Social Media ____

Birthday ____ **H**

~~~~~~~~~~~

Name ____

Address ____

____

____

Phone _______________________ Mobile __________________

E-mail ____

Social Media ____

Birthday ____

~~~~~~~~~~~

Name ____

Address ____

____

____

Phone _______________________ Mobile __________________

E-mail ____

Social Media ____

Birthday ____

Name

Address

Phone   Mobile

E-mail

Social Media

H Birthday

~~~~~~~~~

Name

Address

Phone   Mobile

E-mail

Social Media

Birthday

~~~~~~~~~

Name

Address

Phone   Mobile

E-mail

Social Media

Birthday

Name

Address

Phone   Mobile

E-mail

Social Media

Birthday

~~~~~~~~~~~~

Name

Address

Phone   Mobile

E-mail

Social Media

Birthday

~~~~~~~~~~~~

Name

Address

Phone   Mobile

E-mail

Social Media

Birthday

Name

Address

Phone   Mobile

E-mail

Social Media

Birthday

~~~~~~~~~~

Name

Address

Phone   Mobile

E-mail

Social Media

Birthday

~~~~~~~~~~

Name

Address

Phone   Mobile

E-mail

Social Media

Birthday

Name

Address

Phone   Mobile
E-mail
Social Media
Birthday

~~~~~~~~~

Name

Address

Phone   Mobile
E-mail
Social Media
Birthday

~~~~~~~~~

Name

Address

Phone   Mobile
E-mail
Social Media
Birthday

Name

Address

Phone   Mobile
E-mail
Social Media
Birthday

~~~~~~~~~~

Name

Address

Phone   Mobile
E-mail
Social Media
Birthday

~~~~~~~~~~

Name

Address

Phone   Mobile
E-mail
Social Media
Birthday

Name

Address

Phone   Mobile

E-mail

Social Media

Birthday

~~~~~~~~

J

Name

Address

Phone   Mobile

E-mail

Social Media

Birthday

~~~~~~~~

Name

Address

Phone   Mobile

E-mail

Social Media

Birthday

Name

Address

Phone   Mobile
E-mail
Social Media
Birthday

~~~~~~~~~~

J

Name

Address

Phone   Mobile
E-mail
Social Media
Birthday

~~~~~~~~~~

Name

Address

Phone   Mobile
E-mail
Social Media
Birthday

Name

Address

Phone   Mobile

E-mail

Social Media

Birthday

J

Name

Address

Phone   Mobile

E-mail

Social Media

Birthday

Name

Address

Phone   Mobile

E-mail

Social Media

Birthday

Name

Address

Phone   Mobile

E-mail

Social Media

Birthday

~~~~~~~~~~~

J

Name

Address

Phone   Mobile

E-mail

Social Media

Birthday

~~~~~~~~~~~

Name

Address

Phone   Mobile

E-mail

Social Media

Birthday

Name

Address

Phone   Mobile

E-mail

Social Media

Birthday

~~~~~~~~

Name

Address

Phone   Mobile

E-mail

Social Media

Birthday

~~~~~~~~

Name

Address

Phone   Mobile

E-mail

Social Media

Birthday

Name

Address

Phone   Mobile

E-mail

Social Media

Birthday

~~~~~~~~~

<span style="background:black;color:white">K</span> Name

Address

Phone   Mobile

E-mail

Social Media

Birthday

~~~~~~~~~

Name

Address

Phone   Mobile

E-mail

Social Media

Birthday

Name

Address

Phone   Mobile

E-mail

Social Media

Birthday

~~~~~~~~

Name   **K**

Address

Phone   Mobile

E-mail

Social Media

Birthday

~~~~~~~~

Name

Address

Phone   Mobile

E-mail

Social Media

Birthday

Name

Address

Phone   Mobile

E-mail

Social Media

Birthday

~~~~~~

K Name

Address

Phone   Mobile

E-mail

Social Media

Birthday

~~~~~~

Name

Address

Phone   Mobile

E-mail

Social Media

Birthday

Name

Address

Phone   Mobile

E-mail

Social Media

Birthday

Name

Address

Phone   Mobile

E-mail

Social Media

Birthday

Name

Address

Phone   Mobile

E-mail

Social Media

Birthday

Name

Address

Phone   Mobile

E-mail

Social Media

Birthday

~~~~~~~~

Name

Address

Phone   Mobile

E-mail

Social Media

Birthday

~~~~~~~~

Name

Address

Phone   Mobile

E-mail

Social Media

Birthday

Name

Address

Phone   Mobile

E-mail

Social Media

Birthday

~~~~~~~~

Name

Address

Phone   Mobile

E-mail

Social Media

Birthday

~~~~~~~~

Name

Address

Phone   Mobile

E-mail

Social Media

Birthday

Name

Address

Phone   Mobile

E-mail

Social Media

Birthday

~~~~~~~

Name

Address

Phone   Mobile

E-mail

Social Media

Birthday

~~~~~~~

Name

Address

Phone   Mobile

E-mail

Social Media

Birthday

Name

Address

Phone   Mobile

E-mail

Social Media

Birthday

~~~~~~~~~~

Name

Address

Phone   Mobile

E-mail

Social Media

Birthday

~~~~~~~~~~

Name

Address

Phone   Mobile

E-mail

Social Media

Birthday

M

Name

Address

Phone   Mobile
E-mail
Social Media
Birthday

Name

Address

M

Phone   Mobile
E-mail
Social Media
Birthday

Name

Address

Phone   Mobile
E-mail
Social Media
Birthday

Name

Address

Phone   Mobile

E-mail

Social Media

Birthday

~~~~~~~~

Name

Address

Phone   Mobile

E-mail

Social Media

Birthday

M

~~~~~~~~

Name

Address

Phone   Mobile

E-mail

Social Media

Birthday

Name

Address

Phone   Mobile

E-mail

Social Media

Birthday

~~~~~~~~~

Name

Address

M

Phone   Mobile

E-mail

Social Media

Birthday

~~~~~~~~~

Name

Address

Phone   Mobile

E-mail

Social Media

Birthday

Name

Address

Phone   Mobile

E-mail

Social Media

Birthday

~~~~~~~~

Name

Address

Phone   Mobile

E-mail

Social Media

Birthday

~~~~~~~~

Name

Address

Phone   Mobile

E-mail

Social Media

Birthday

Name

Address

Phone   Mobile

E-mail

Social Media

Birthday

~~~~~~~~~~

Name

Address

N Phone   Mobile

E-mail

Social Media

Birthday

~~~~~~~~~~

Name

Address

Phone   Mobile

E-mail

Social Media

Birthday

Name

Address

Phone   Mobile

E-mail

Social Media

Birthday

~~~~~~~

Name

Address

Phone   Mobile

E-mail

Social Media

Birthday

N

~~~~~~~

Name

Address

Phone   Mobile

E-mail

Social Media

Birthday

Name

Address

Phone   Mobile

E-mail

Social Media

Birthday

~~~~~~~~~~

Name

Address

N Phone   Mobile

E-mail

Social Media

Birthday

~~~~~~~~~~

Name

Address

Phone   Mobile

E-mail

Social Media

Birthday

Name

Address

Phone   Mobile

E-mail

Social Media

Birthday

~~~~~~~

Name

Address

Phone   Mobile

E-mail

Social Media

Birthday

~~~~~~~

Name

Address

Phone   Mobile

E-mail

Social Media

Birthday

Name

Address

Phone   Mobile

E-mail

Social Media

Birthday

~~~~~~~~~~

Name

Address

Phone   Mobile

O E-mail

Social Media

Birthday

~~~~~~~~~~

Name

Address

Phone   Mobile

E-mail

Social Media

Birthday

Name

Address

Phone   Mobile

E-mail

Social Media

Birthday

Name

Address

Phone   Mobile

E-mail

Social Media

Birthday

Name

Address

Phone   Mobile

E-mail

Social Media

Birthday

Name

Address

Phone   Mobile

E-mail

Social Media

Birthday

~~~~~~~~

Name

Address

Phone   Mobile

O E-mail

Social Media

Birthday

~~~~~~~~

Name

Address

Phone   Mobile

E-mail

Social Media

Birthday

Name

Address

Phone   Mobile

E-mail

Social Media

Birthday

~~~~~~~~~~

Name

Address

Phone   Mobile

E-mail

Social Media

Birthday

~~~~~~~~~~

Name

Address

Phone   Mobile

E-mail

Social Media

Birthday

Name

Address

Phone   Mobile

E-mail

Social Media

Birthday

~~~~~~~~~

Name

Address

Phone   Mobile

E-mail

P Social Media

Birthday

~~~~~~~~~

Name

Address

Phone   Mobile

E-mail

Social Media

Birthday

Name

Address

Phone   Mobile

E-mail

Social Media

Birthday

~~~~~~~~~

Name

Address

Phone   Mobile

E-mail

Social Media

Birthday

~~~~~~~~~

Name

Address

Phone   Mobile

E-mail

Social Media

Birthday

Name

Address

Phone   Mobile

E-mail

Social Media

Birthday

~~~~~~~~~~

Name

Address

Phone   Mobile

E-mail

Social Media

Birthday

~~~~~~~~~~

Name

Address

Phone   Mobile

E-mail

Social Media

Birthday

Name

Address

Phone   Mobile

E-mail

Social Media

Birthday

Name

Address

Phone   Mobile

E-mail

Social Media

Birthday

Q

Name

Address

Phone   Mobile

E-mail

Social Media

Birthday

Name

Address

Phone   Mobile

E-mail

Social Media

Birthday

~~~~~~~~~

Name

Address

Phone   Mobile

E-mail

Social Media

Birthday

Q

~~~~~~~~~

Name

Address

Phone   Mobile

E-mail

Social Media

Birthday

Name

Address

Phone   Mobile

E-mail

Social Media

Birthday

~~~~~~~~~~

Name

Address

Phone   Mobile

E-mail

Social Media

Birthday

Q

~~~~~~~~~~

Name

Address

Phone   Mobile

E-mail

Social Media

Birthday

Name

Address

Phone   Mobile

E-mail

Social Media

Birthday

~~~~~~~

Name

Address

Phone   Mobile

E-mail

Social Media

Birthday

Q

~~~~~~~

Name

Address

Phone   Mobile

E-mail

Social Media

Birthday

Name

Address

Phone   Mobile

E-mail

Social Media

Birthday

~~~~~~~~

Name

Address

Phone   Mobile

E-mail

Social Media

Birthday

~~~~~~~~

R

Name

Address

Phone   Mobile

E-mail

Social Media

Birthday

Name

Address

Phone   Mobile

E-mail

Social Media

Birthday

~~~~~~~

Name

Address

Phone   Mobile

E-mail

Social Media

Birthday

R

~~~~~~~

Name

Address

Phone   Mobile

E-mail

Social Media

Birthday

Name

Address

Phone   Mobile

E-mail

Social Media

Birthday

~~~~~~~

Name

Address

Phone   Mobile

E-mail

Social Media

Birthday

~~~~~~~

Name

Address

Phone   Mobile

E-mail

Social Media

Birthday

Name

Address

Phone   Mobile

E-mail

Social Media

Birthday

~~~~~~~~~~

Name

Address

Phone   Mobile

E-mail

Social Media

Birthday

~~~~~~~~~~

R

Name

Address

Phone   Mobile

E-mail

Social Media

Birthday

Name

Address

Phone   Mobile
E-mail
Social Media
Birthday

~~~~~~~~~~

Name

Address

Phone   Mobile
E-mail
Social Media
Birthday

~~~~~~~~~~

S

Name

Address

Phone   Mobile
E-mail
Social Media
Birthday

Name

Address

Phone   Mobile

E-mail

Social Media

Birthday

~~~~~~~

Name

Address

Phone   Mobile

E-mail

Social Media

Birthday

~~~~~~~

S Name

Address

Phone   Mobile

E-mail

Social Media

Birthday

Name

Address

Phone   Mobile

E-mail

Social Media

Birthday

~~~~~~~~~~

Name

Address

Phone   Mobile

E-mail

Social Media

Birthday

~~~~~~~~~~

S

Name

Address

Phone   Mobile

E-mail

Social Media

Birthday

Name

Address

Phone   Mobile

E-mail

Social Media

Birthday

~~~~~~~~~~

Name

Address

Phone   Mobile

E-mail

Social Media

Birthday

~~~~~~~~~~

S Name

Address

Phone   Mobile

E-mail

Social Media

Birthday

Name

Address

Phone   Mobile

E-mail

Social Media

Birthday

~~~~~~~~~

Name

Address

Phone   Mobile

E-mail

Social Media

Birthday

~~~~~~~~~

Name

Address

Phone   Mobile

E-mail

Social Media

Birthday

Name ____

Address ____

____

Phone ________________________ Mobile __________

E-mail ____

Social Media ____________________________________

Birthday ____

~~~~~~~~~~

Name ____

Address ____

____

Phone ________________________ Mobile __________

E-mail ____

Social Media ____________________________________

Birthday ____

~~~~~~~~~~

Name ____

Address ____

____

Phone ________________________ Mobile __________

E-mail ____

Social Media ____________________________________

Birthday ____

Name

Address

Phone   Mobile

E-mail

Social Media

Birthday

~~~~~~~

Name

Address

Phone   Mobile

E-mail

Social Media

Birthday

~~~~~~~

Name

Address

Phone   Mobile

E-mail

Social Media

Birthday

Name

Address

Phone   Mobile

E-mail

Social Media

Birthday

~~~~~~~~

Name

Address

Phone   Mobile

E-mail

Social Media

Birthday

~~~~~~~~

Name

Address

Phone   Mobile

E-mail

Social Media

Birthday

Name

Address

Phone   Mobile

E-mail

Social Media

Birthday

~~~~~~~~~~

Name

Address

Phone   Mobile

E-mail

Social Media

Birthday

~~~~~~~~~~

Name

Address

Phone   Mobile

E-mail

Social Media

Birthday

Name

Address

Phone   Mobile

E-mail

Social Media

Birthday

Name

Address

Phone   Mobile

E-mail

Social Media

Birthday

Name

Address

Phone   Mobile

E-mail

Social Media

Birthday

Name

Address

Phone   Mobile

E-mail

Social Media

Birthday

~~~~~~~~~~~

Name

Address

Phone   Mobile

E-mail

Social Media

Birthday

~~~~~~~~~~~

Name

Address

Phone   Mobile

E-mail

Social Media

Birthday

Name

Address

Phone   Mobile

E-mail

Social Media

Birthday

~~~~~~~~~

Name

Address

Phone   Mobile

E-mail

Social Media

Birthday

~~~~~~~~~

Name

Address

U

Phone   Mobile

E-mail

Social Media

Birthday

Name

Address

Phone   Mobile

E-mail

Social Media

Birthday

~~~~~~~

Name

Address

Phone   Mobile

E-mail

Social Media

Birthday

~~~~~~~

Name

Address

Phone   Mobile

E-mail

Social Media

Birthday

Name

Address

Phone   Mobile
E-mail
Social Media
Birthday

~~~~~~~~~

Name

Address

Phone   Mobile
E-mail
Social Media
Birthday

~~~~~~~~~

Name

Address

V

Phone   Mobile
E-mail
Social Media
Birthday

Name

Address

Phone   Mobile

E-mail

Social Media

Birthday

~~~~~~~

Name

Address

Phone   Mobile

E-mail

Social Media

Birthday

~~~~~~~

Name

Address

Phone   Mobile

E-mail

Social Media

Birthday

Name

Address

Phone   Mobile

E-mail

Social Media

Birthday

~~~~~~~~~~

Name

Address

Phone   Mobile

E-mail

Social Media

Birthday

~~~~~~~~~~

Name

Address

V Phone   Mobile

E-mail

Social Media

Birthday

Name

Address

Phone   Mobile

E-mail

Social Media

Birthday

~~~~~~

Name

Address

Phone   Mobile

E-mail

Social Media

Birthday

~~~~~~

Name

Address

Phone   Mobile

E-mail

Social Media

Birthday

Name

Address

Phone   Mobile

E-mail

Social Media

Birthday

~~~~~~~~

Name

Address

Phone   Mobile

E-mail

Social Media

Birthday

~~~~~~~~

Name

Address

Phone   Mobile

E-mail

Social Media

Birthday

Name

Address

Phone   Mobile

E-mail

Social Media

Birthday

~~~~~~~~

Name

Address

Phone   Mobile

E-mail

Social Media

Birthday

~~~~~~~~

Name

Address

Phone   Mobile

E-mail

Social Media

Birthday

Name

Address

Phone   Mobile

E-mail

Social Media

Birthday

~~~~~~~~~~

Name

Address

Phone   Mobile

E-mail

Social Media

Birthday

~~~~~~~~~~

Name

Address

Phone   Mobile

E-mail

Social Media

Birthday

Name

Address

Phone   Mobile

E-mail

Social Media

Birthday

~~~~~~~

Name

Address

Phone   Mobile

E-mail

Social Media

Birthday

~~~~~~~

Name

Address

Phone   Mobile

E-mail

Social Media

Birthday

X

Name

Address

Phone   Mobile

E-mail

Social Media

Birthday

~~~~~~~

Name

Address

Phone   Mobile

E-mail

Social Media

Birthday

~~~~~~~

Name

Address

Phone   Mobile

E-mail

X Social Media

Birthday

Name

Address

Phone   Mobile

E-mail

Social Media

Birthday

~~~~~~~~~~

Name

Address

Phone   Mobile

E-mail

Social Media

Birthday

~~~~~~~~~~

Name

Address

Phone   Mobile

E-mail

Social Media

Birthday

X

Name

Address

Phone   Mobile

E-mail

Social Media

Birthday

~~~~~~~

Name

Address

Phone   Mobile

E-mail

Social Media

Birthday

~~~~~~~

Name

Address

Phone   Mobile

E-mail

X Social Media

Birthday

Name

Address

Phone   Mobile

E-mail

Social Media

Birthday

~~~~~~

Name

Address

Phone   Mobile

E-mail

Social Media

Birthday

~~~~~~

Name

Address

Phone   Mobile

E-mail

Social Media

Birthday

Name

Address

Phone   Mobile

E-mail

Social Media

Birthday

Name

Address

Phone   Mobile

E-mail

Social Media

Birthday

Name

Address

Phone   Mobile

E-mail

Social Media

Birthday

Name

Address

Phone   Mobile

E-mail

Social Media

Birthday

~~~~~~~

Name

Address

Phone   Mobile

E-mail

Social Media

Birthday

~~~~~~~

Name

Address

Phone   Mobile

E-mail

Social Media

Birthday

Name

Address

Phone   Mobile

E-mail

Social Media

Birthday

~~~~~~~

Name

Address

Phone   Mobile

E-mail

Social Media

Birthday

~~~~~~~

Name

Address

Phone   Mobile

E-mail

Social Media

Birthday

Name

Address

Phone   Mobile

E-mail

Social Media

Birthday

~~~~~~~~

Name

Address

Phone   Mobile

E-mail

Social Media

Birthday

~~~~~~~~

Name

Address

Phone   Mobile

E-mail

Social Media

Birthday

Z

Name

Address

Phone   Mobile

E-mail

Social Media

Birthday

~~~~~~~

Name

Address

Phone   Mobile

E-mail

Social Media

Birthday

~~~~~~~

Name

Address

Phone   Mobile

E-mail

Social Media

Birthday

Name

Address

Phone   Mobile

E-mail

Social Media

Birthday

~~~~~~~~~~

Name

Address

Phone   Mobile

E-mail

Social Media

Birthday

~~~~~~~~~~

Name

Address

Phone   Mobile

E-mail

Social Media

Birthday

Z

Name

Address

Phone   Mobile
E-mail
Social Media
Birthday

~~~~~~~~~

Name

Address

Phone   Mobile
E-mail
Social Media
Birthday

~~~~~~~~~

Name

Address

Phone   Mobile
E-mail
Social Media
Birthday

Z

NOTE

NOTE

Made in the USA
Monee, IL
07 July 2026

56551564R00066